Quick Changeover in the OR

Gerard Leone
Richard D. Rahn

Flow Publishing, Inc.
Boulder, Colorado

Quick Changeover in the OR
By Gerard Leone, Richard Rahn

Published by:

Flow Publishing Inc.
7690 Watonga Way
Boulder, Colorado 80303
(303) 494-4693
www.flowpublishing.com
contact@flowpublishing.com

ISBN-13 978-0-9833839-0-1

Table of Contents

Introduction

Most hospitals across the United States are feeling the financial pressures. There never seem to be enough resources to deliver as much care as required by the community and with the quality the hospital considers the community deserves. Staff members and administrators stretch themselves to the max to take care of all the patients that require care. The gravity of the situation is all the more evident in the Perioperative Services Department. This is a department that uses more resources than any other place in the hospital. The resources used in the Perioperative Services Department are some of the most expensive in the entire hospital, making the financial pressures even more critical.

One additional pressure the Perioperative Department faces is competition. Hospitals in general do not see themselves as competing with other hospitals, unless they are in a crowded market. It is unlikely that a parent will drive a few extra miles with a child with a broken arm in search of a better deal. It just does not happen. This is not the case with the OR. According to the CDC, only 58% of all surgeries take place in a hospital. Then, there is the pressure from overseas hospitals and surgery centers offering much lower rates for private payers.

In this environment, the Perioperative Services Department must look everywhere for improvements, from acquiring, storing, issuing, using, and charging for supplies to maximizing the utilization of one the most expensive fixed assets in the entire hospital, the OR Suite.

To maximize the utilization of every OR Suite while increasing quality of care, Leadership must look beyond the traditional tools and embrace the power of Lean thinking. One of the most widespread tools in the Lean toolbox is Quick Changeover, known in the manufacturing circles as SMED, or Single Minute Exchange of Dies.

This book describes the Quick Changeover tool in detail from the OR perspective and for OR staff members. However, the contents of this book apply to all procedure rooms, as well as patient rooms in the hospital.

The objective of this book is to:

- Provide you with an understanding of Quick Changeover and its application to the OR Suite.

- Supply you all the necessary definitions, especially of Internal Changeover Steps and External Changeover Steps.

- Describe the Quick Changeover steps of Separating, Converting, and Streamlining.

- Provide you with examples of the key tools, like the Standard Work Definition, Spaghetti Diagrams, and checklists.

- Place Quick Changeover within the largest context of a Lean initiative with the management of medical supplies, a Lean Management System, and Kaizen.

This book, like all the other books in this series, will deliver much more value when its content is discussed with your team members as you work on actual OR Suite Changeover optimization projects.

We hope you enjoy the book and tell us about your projects.

Chapter 1: Benefits of Quick Changeover for the OR Suite

Like any fixed asset, an OR Suite delivers value only when in use. We must, however, qualify the "use" of an OR Suite. The fact that activity is taking place inside the OR Suite does not directly mean this fixed asset is delivering value. During the time the OR Suite is being cleaned, set up, repaired, inspected, or any of the long list of activities that we label as *non-value adding*, it is "in use" but it is not delivering value. For the OR Suite to deliver value, it must be involved in an actual patient procedure. This is true for any procedure room or other asset throughout the hospital.

This appears to be a minor or even obvious point, but it is a critical one. You might hear "Our hospital is not the preferred place of practice for the community surgeons because we do too few procedures per day." If your reaction is "How can this be? I am working myself silly in this place" then you are not yet looking at the issue through Lean eyes. Administrators may also approach the issue the wrong way by thinking that this is "somebody's fault" and all that is needed is some more management pressure. We need to make this point as clear as we can:

It is NOT the people, it is the process.

If you have personnel issues, put this book down and go solve your people problem and come back later when you can trust your people. We must start from a place of believing that we all want to be a part of something good; nobody wants to be member of the losing team.

To keep the OR Suite delivering value, you must maximize the time it is performing procedures, or looking at the issue from the other side you must minimize the time the suite is NOT performing procedures. Any time an OR Suite is not involved in a procedure, it is either being changed over or it is idle. For the purpose of our discussion, we are not going to worry about idle time, since it tends to reveal a low procedure volume. If you had *that* problem, you would not be reading this book. So, we are ready to make this pivotal statement:

To maximize the delivery of value, you must minimize changeover time.

Minimizing OR Suite changeover time will result in a series of benefits derived from maximizing the delivery of value. Some of the benefits include improved patient throughput and patient flow, improved asset and staff productivity, improved quality of care, improved on-start times, and increased revenue for the hospital.

Improved Patient Throughput. By reducing the amount of time spent on changeovers, you convert the non-value-adding time of changeover to the value -adding time of procedures. Let's do some quick math. Think of a Perioperative Services Department that has 8 OR Suites that perform 40 procedures per day with average procedure times of 90 minutes and average changeover times of 45 minutes. These numbers indicate that this department spends 40 x 45 minutes on changeovers, for a grand total of 1,800 minutes/day. What would it happen if your team was able to remove 15 minutes from each changeover, bringing the average down to 30 min? The new grand total would be 40 x 30 equaling 1,200 minutes for a net gain of 600 minutes that can be reinvested in procedures. Considering an average of 90 minutes per procedure, you are looking at almost 7 more procedures per day. Some of this time savings should be reinvested in better quality procedures.

Improved Asset and Staff Productivity. The definition of the term productivity is sometimes subject to argument. The simplest and most effective way to look at productivity is as a ratio of output-to-input. In other words, how much value do you get from the resources you contribute? By increasing patient throughput, you are increasing the numerator of the ratio without affecting the denominator. For staff members that get nervous that "they are trying to make us work harder", we recommend you stop for a second and ask yourself if you became an OR Nurse or an Instrument Tech to wait around for the room to become available, or for the case cart to arrive, or to go hunting to complete a case cart. You entered this this noble field to take care of patients.

Improved Quality of Care. By reducing the amount of time you spend on changeovers, you can spend more time taking care of patients. This does not always mean to push more volume all the way to the max. Stop and ask yourself "How do I improve quality of care?" The answer is "By spending more time on quality". This may come in the form of devoting the time to the pre-procedure checklist, applying the enzymatic foam to the outgoing instrument set, doing a proper post-procedure instrument count, or the many best practices we know improve quality. All those best practices require time, time that can be recovered from wasteful changeover steps.

Improved On-Time Starts. Most hospitals measure on-time starts only by the first case of the day. That may be the current state of affairs, but as more hospitals look at improving the efficiency of their operations, measuring *all* on-time starts will become a more widespread practice. By having a predictable and repeatable changeover procedure, you can assure staff and surgeons, that by the time they deliver the patient to PACU, and go see the next patient in pre-surg, the room will be ready to go. This may sound next to impossible as you read this, but do not be discouraged by the fact that the answers are not available right now. Part of the "Kaizen Spirit" is to shoot for perfection and reap the benefits along the way.

Increased Revenue for the Hospital. It is a pretty straightforward conclusion: if you continue with the math we started above, the increased number of procedures will result in increased revenue for the hospital. We must now caution you one more time that you need to think about reinvesting some of the time you recover on improved quality. A few years ago, we helped a team at a client hospital complete a project that could save the equivalent of $2.2 million in RN time. When the team proudly presented their project to the Executive team, after the applause the CFO raised his hand to make the following statement: "As you know, none of this is real money, unless we get rid of a bunch of nurses. Well, I am here to tell you that this is not money I want. This time must be reinvested in making the nurses job more meaningful and in taking better care of our patients. We will find actual cash in the many other projects we have in the Continuous Improvement database."

Every hospital must stay focused on financial performance to remain viable. Asset utilization is one of the key aspects of a hospital's financial performance. Quick Changeover can represent a multi-million dollar opportunity, as it will enable all procedure rooms to deliver more value to patients. This is also true for other stakeholders like surgeons, nurses and instrument techs, as they will be able to spend more time taking care of patients and less time in non-value-adding activities. In the coming chapters we will be discussing the actual process for achieving these benefits.

Chapter 1: Knowledge Check

The OR Suite and the OR staff are delivering value during a Changeover.

☐ True
☐ False

The Main Benefits of Quick Changeover in the OR Suite are:

☐ Improved Patient throughput.
☐ Higher Fixed Asset Productivity
☐ Increased Staff Productivity
☐ Better Quality of Care
☐ Improved On-time Starts
☐ Higher Revenue for the Hospital
☐ All of the above

The Quick OR Suite Changeover opportunity is small (from a financial perspective) and can be measured in only thousands of dollars.

☐ True
☐ False

14 Quick Changeover in the OR

Chapter 2: A Brief History of the Quick Changeover Method

The time was the late 1950's. Struggling to survive after near-bankruptcy in the early part of the decade, the Toyota Motor Company had dedicated itself to rebuilding, and to the ideal of "Kaizen" or continuous improvement in all of its processes. One of the challenges they faced was excessively long changeover times on their large presses, the machines that stamp out body parts. They had discovered that one of their competitors was able to change over the identical machine in three hours from one part to another, as compared to Toyota's current best time of six hours. They had assigned the task of reducing the time to at least equal the competition to a young engineer named Shigeo Shingo, and after several months of team effort he was ready to report the results.

"We had achieved our goal," Shingo reported in his autobiography, "and we were proud to be able to report success. However, after the initial congratulations from the plant manager, he gave us our next assignment. What I want you to do, he said, is to now reduce the time from three hours to three minutes. We all thought he was literally crazy." After the initial shock wore off, and because he couldn't say no, the wheels began to turn in Shingo's mind, and the light bulb went on when he realized that the goal was not to eliminate three hours of labor time, but to reduce the time that the expensive piece of equipment was unavailable for use. This insight was the beginning of what is now called SMED, *Single Minute Exchange of Dies*, or quick changeover in less than 10 minutes.

Roll time forward about 20 years. Americans in the late 1970's and early 1980's began to take learning trips to Japan, to try to uncover the secrets of the Japanese Economic Miracle. One of the leaders of these executive tours, Norman Bodek, returned with a copy (in badly translated English) of a book titled *The SMED System* by Shigeo Shingo. Copies were distributed, an much improved translation was done, and this book was one of the first exposures by Westerners to the Quick Changeover methodology, and also launched Bodek's company Productivity Press.

SMED is a rather strange term, even for manufacturing folks, and we won't be using it in this book, preferring instead the term *Quick Changeover*. The methods, however, apply well to our needs in a hospital environment. As you'll see, the Quick Chaangeover steps are also very common-sense and easy to understand, although to get the maximum result some creative thinking and effort will be needed.

The term "Single Minute" really means "less than 10 minutes", and this was actually achieved by Shingo with his stamping presses. Is a 10 minute changeover in an OR suite possible? The answer is probably yes. Is it desirable? Maybe not. If this is our goal, and you simply *had to do it*, then you could come up with a process that could achieve that goal. We sent a man to the moon, so we think you could changeover an OR suite in less than 10 minutes. The cost of doing so, however, may outweigh the benefits. The good news is that by applying the Quick Changeover methodology you can make major improvements at very low cost. Let's take advantage of these opportunities first before we get too ambitious, or set artificial goals for ourselves.

Today the Quick Changeover method is one of the core methods of Lean, and practiced by thousands of organizations around the globe. It will also soon be a core competency of the Lean Hospital and the perioperative services department.

Chapter 2: Knowledge Check

The term SMED is an acronym for:

☐ Shingo Manufacturing Equipment
Development

☐ Single Machine Efficiency Device

☐ Single Minute Exchange of Dies

☐ Trick Question: SMED is the Japanese Word
for "Quick Changeover"

The expression "Single Minute" in Quick Changeover means:

☐ Less than a minute

☐ Around a minute but no more than 2 minutes

☐ Less than 10 minutes

☐ Less than 1 hour

True or False: Unless you are able to reduce a changeover to "single minute" range, your Quick Changeover project has not been successful.

☐ True

☐ False

Chapter 3: Getting Ready for Quick Changeover

One of the keys to success for any Lean improvement project (Kaizen Event) is to do as much as possible ahead of time. Logically, if you wait until the actual event to do something that could have already been done, you are consuming valuable Kaizen time that could be applied to brainstorming, implementation, training, documentation and other necessary aspects of the effort. Not coincidentally, this recommendation is also the first phase of a Quick Changeover project, called *Separating Internal from External*, to be discussed in the next chapter. An external step is a work step that can be done while the process is working. In the case of an OR, an external step can be done while the prior procedure is still going on. An internal step, the opposite, *cannot* be done while the prior procedure is going on, and can only be done when the OR Suite is not in use. More on this later.

This chapter discusses the tasks that can and should be done ahead of time, prior to a Quick Changeover conversion Kaizen event. A failure to complete this work ahead of time can jeopardize the success of the event, since some of the action items are quite time-consuming.

STANDARD WORK DEFINITION

LEAN HOSPITAL

Value Stream _____
Process _____
SWD Name _____
Date Created _____
Revision _____

Order	Description of Work Performed	Supplies	NVA Y/N	Divisible Y/N	Int / Ext	Equip. Time	Staff Time	Transp Time	TGM Check	Self-check Description

20 Quick Changeover in the OR

Document the Current State

Task 1 for our advanced preparation is to *Document the Current State*. You need to understand in detail how OR Suite changeovers are being done today, warts and all. The way things are done today is called the *Current State*, and it is important to capture a realistic picture of the existing changeover process as a foundation for the analysis and improvement ideas to come. You will need a detailed step-by-step documentation of the process, by skill set (nurse, tech, ORA, etc.). Above is an example of the form used for this purpose. The form itself, called the Standard Work Definition, can be downloaded from the Lean Hospital website in spreadsheet format; see the chapter in this book on Standard Work for a more in-depth explanation of this form, and how to fill it out.

Could the current state be documented during the Kaizen event itself? Yes, but we don't recommend waiting. We don't want to take the risk of something going wrong, and delaying the creative work of the Kaizen event itself. Let's make sure that the Current State is documented beforehand.

Think in terms of shadowing a nurse or tech around during the changeover process. There are three critical pieces of information you will need to capture:

1. Document the work steps. For each logical "chunk" of work, write down a short description of the work step. You should be fairly detailed. A typical work step might be: "Push case cart to outgoing dirty elevator and return".

2. Document the time required to complete the previous work step. You are interested in an average time, and you don't need to get hung up over the fact that the times will vary somewhat from person to person, or case to case. If possible, take a sample of times with different people, and use the average. In most cases it will be sufficient to document the times in whole minutes, instead of seconds. Using our previous example, you might find that the time required to move a case cart (and come back) averages 3 minutes.

3. Document the "Self Check Description". For each of the work steps, ask yourself the question "Could a person trying to do a good job do this step wrong?" People will make mistakes, and if a mistake is possible then you need to document the need for an inspection or check, before you move on to the next work step. In our previous example, it may be possible to drop the cart off in the wrong place, outside of designated parking lanes. The Self Check Description might therefore say "Verify that the case cart is parked in the formally dedicated locations, within the taped lines. Wash hands after dropping off cart."

Note: if it is *not* possible to make a mistake on a work step (or if the possibility of a mistake is very remote) then you can call this work step *mistake-proofed*, and a check is not required. Generally, however, Murphy's Law rules, and if something can go wrong, it will.

These are the most important columns to complete on the form, but you should read the Chapter 8 on Standard Work and Quick Changeover for a discussion of the data collection in more detail.

Shadowing a person or persons can be tiring and also inaccurate, so we recommend that you video the changeover process instead. Once you've captured the changeover in a video file, you can observe and review each work step off-line by watching the video. If a step is not clearly understood in the video, you can also get the help of the staff person to explain what is being done. Use a camera that will also record the time, and this will make it much easier to capture the work time accurately.

When workers know they are being filmed, they will typically do one of two things, depending on the work culture of your hospital. In a more highly structured or unionized environment, people may slow down, under the belief that attempts are being made to change the expected work pace, or get staff members to work faster. On the other hand, if the staff members feel that they are being evaluated, they may tend to speed up. Neither case is desirable, so it will be important to encourage your video subjects to "act naturally", and reassure them that you are documenting the work itself, and not the person, and that you want accurate work steps and realistic work times.

A video will be extremely useful in capturing detailed work steps, but you also want to collect a sample of *overall* changeover times, over a period of weeks or months. If you are lucky, you already have an electronic system that is capturing this information, but be careful. You are interested in the elapsed time from the end of the prior procedure to the time that the OR suite is available for the next one. When the next one actually starts is a separate issue. The suite may be available but the procedure not started, for a variety of reasons. Find out how "ending" times are captured in your system, to ensure that you are capturing the time interval that you actually want. In

| PROCEDURE 1 | C/O | IDLE | PROCEDURE 2 | C/O | ....⇨ |

most cases you don't want the start time of the next procedure.

If you don't have an electronic system, or if the system cannot easily collect the data you want, it may be necessary to put in place a manual log. You don't want a manual system to be too onerous, but you do want to have a reasonably large data set of actual changeover times.

Be prepared to do Quick Changeover training.

Every formal Kaizen event will usually include some formal training in the Lean tool being used. You can't assume that everyone on the Kaizen team, especially when you are new to Lean, will have knowledge or experience in Quick Changeover methods. Even with a more experienced team, a refresher doesn't hurt, and it helps to ensure that everyone is on the same page and speaking the same language. This training will be to-the-point, practical and concise, and with a goal of completing it in an hour or less. Remember that most of the training will come by *doing*, under the guidance of a mentor and team leader, so you don't need to be too concerned that the formal training is not sufficient.

You will need both training materials and a trainer to complete this step, which is usually done on the morning of the first day of the Kaizen event. Your preparation action item is to make sure that these items will be available. One advantage of working with an outside Lean consultant is that this will normally become their responsibility. Eventually, however, your hospital should have internal resources that can teach this topic well. Use this book as a training guide.

Schedule the Kaizen Event with Enough Lead-time

Make sure that this point is made very clear to all members of the Quick Changeover Kaizen event: during the event itself their time is committed to the event 100%. One of the important keys to success is to focus as a team on the objective at hand. Since everyone already has a regular job, those normal job duties will need to be covered by others during the Kaizen event. This will require some planning and scheduling, so give your prospective team members at least a few weeks (or more) to make these arrangements.

Organize the Kaizen Event Supplies and Materials

It would be a shame to waste precious Kaizen event time looking for supplies and materials, or making facilities arrangements. Here's a checklist of the supplies, materials and other organizational items you'll need to arrange ahead of time.

A meeting place. Most of your time should be spent in the "gemba", i.e. where the work is done, but you will need a meeting space for your team. A conference room or office that can hold 4-6 people is ideal.

Meeting place equipment. A computer projector, a flip chart or two, working markers, sticky notes, pens and paper are all good items to have on-hand. If participants have laptops these can be used, but otherwise provide access at least two computers (that can also play our video files). Finally, it's very handy to have a printer easily available.

Provide refreshments. You don't want the team wandering away at lunchtime; try to keep them together by providing lunch. Coffee and other drinks during the day will also be needed.

Other supplies. You may be doing some timing, so a few stopwatches would be good to have available. You have done your video work earlier, but videos of the "Future State" may also be a good idea, so have a video camera available. As you gain experience in these events, you will develop the ability to foresee what supplies you may need like floor tape, boards and signage, a cart, etc. Use the more experienced team members, or your Lean consultant for this.

With these preparation steps completed you should be in great shape for a successful Quick Changeover Kaizen Event, where you can focus a majority of your time on process improvements and the Future State. In the next chapters we will discuss the approach to take to Quick Changeover process improvement, and how to structure the analysis and team discussion.

Chapter 3: Knowledge Check

When documenting the Current State, it is important to:

- ☐ Wait until the actual Quick Changeover event, in order to collect fresh data.
- ☐ Use the best estimates of the OR staff since the actual changeovers will be impossible to observe.
- ☐ Complete this task ahead of time, in order to free up time during the event for improvements.
- ☐ Not let the staff know what you are doing, since that might cause them to slow down or speed up.

When documenting the work steps and times for the Current State, you should:

- ☐ Use a blank sheet of paper and a pencil only, in accordance with "Lean" methods.
- ☐ Make sure that you time the best and fastest staff member, in order to document the ideal process.
- ☐ Use the Standard Work Definition form, to ensure that all of the required data elements are considered.
- ☐ Document work steps only, since times will be impossible to measure and are highly variable.

During the actual Quick Changeover event, some formal training in the subject will be needed. How should you plan for that need?

☐ Buy a book on Quick Changeover and require that all team members read it ahead of time.

☐ If in-house expertise is available, use it. Otherwise skip the formal training and get right to work.

☐ High quality videos are available. Plan to watch one on Day 1 of the event as a team.

☐ If in-house expertise is available, use it. Otherwise rely on a Lean mentor to conduct the training and/or train the trainers for future events.

Chapter 4: Separating Internal and External Steps

Let's bring back the definitions of Internal Changeover steps versus External Changeover steps from Chapter 3 and make them formal:

> *An Internal Changeover step can only be done while there is no procedure taking place in the OR Suite.*

This means that the OR Suite must be empty of patients while the Internal Changeover steps are being performed. A very typical example would be the post-procedure room cleanup or a terminal cleaning. While the cleaning crew is wiping the floors, the tables, the anesthesia machine, and the bair hugger, no procedure can be taking place concurrently.

This is the worst type of changeover step, because it encumbers the room and prevents clinicians from taking care of a patient. One of the goals for your Kaizen team will be the reduction of internal steps. Of course there are internal steps that cannot, and should not, be eliminated, like all cleaning steps. Then your team must look for ways to minimize their duration.

Let's stay with the cleaning for a short while. How long does it take to wipe the room and all the equipment? How many staff member perform that duty? What is the post-cleaning dwell time for the chemicals you use? Clearly, during that time no patient should be in the room. That makes these events *internal changeover* steps. Let's now have another look at the cleaning steps. Have you tried increasing the crew size? Usually, increasing the crew size decreases cleaning time more than proportionally, by reducing the waste of motion. Then again, maybe your OR Suite layout does not allow for that. Have you diagrammed the physical movement of the cleaning crew? Their procedures may not be the most efficient and they may be jumping from location to location and doing too much walking. What about the chemicals you use? Assuming they are mixed properly, do they have the optimal dwell time for your OR Suite? As an example, bleach products have approximately a 15 minutes of dwell time. The point of this discussion is to guide you and your team in the direction of eliminating internal changeover steps, and when that is not possible, look to minimize their duration.

There will be some steps you will identify as internal steps and immediately say "That step is necessary and cannot go away, so let's move on". Hold on a second there. That you and the team may not have the answer right now, it does not mean you should ignore savings opportunities. If there is a chemical that could reduce dwell time but you and the team have no immediate access or knowledge, document that step in a "to be researched" folder or database so the team or somebody else can go back to this opportunity without having to start from scratch.

Let's now define an External Changeover step:

> *An External Changeover step can be done while the prior procedure is taking place.*

This means that while the hip replacement on Mrs. Smith is taking place, you can be performing some changeover steps in anticipation of Mr. Brown's knee replacement. If your case carts come incomplete by design with no sutures, the sutures must be obtained prior to the start of the case. The sutures could be obtained by the OR Nurse, delaying the start of the case, or they could be gathered by an OR Assistant and placed on the case cart in accordance with the preference card. In this manner, the OR Nurse can work on the prior case while the ORA obtains the sutures. The search, hopefully short, for the right suture and the placement on the case cart in the right location was performed external to the case. As far as changeover steps go, this is preferable for it does not encumber the OR Suite, allowing for more time to take care of patients.

One of your team's goals will be to document every step of work in the changeover procedure from beginning to end and to identify these external steps. For that you and the team will need to practice identifying steps of work, documenting them, and classifying them as internal or external. Since nobody was born with this knowledge, we recommend that you practice this skill by diligently observing a few changeovers to document its steps. Do not try to improve anything just yet, just observe the work, identify steps, document the steps and classify them into internal and external.

Let's practice on the table below. These steps are in no specific order and they relate to an actual changeover plan for a Perioperative Services department. Try classifying the steps into internal and external in the right-hand column.

Step	I/E
Apply enzymatic foam to "dirty" set	
Deliver "dirty" case cart to elevator	
Retrieve case cart for next case	
Retrieve backup instrument set and supplies from case cart and place in "backup" shelf	
Move backup set and supplies from "backup" shelf to "return" shelf	
Wipe positioning devices	
Setup back table	
Tear down room	
Deliver dirty linen to utility room	
Clean OR Suite after procedure	
Find C-Arm and bring to OR Suite	
Complete cart with preference supplies from Sterile Core	
Find positioning devices	

If you identified a step as external, you are saying that such step can be done outside of the OR Suite and concurrently with the prior step. Do not worry yet about how long it takes, we are leaving that for Chapter 6 on Streamlining.

If you marked a step as internal, you are conversely saying that such step encumbers the OR Suite and cannot be performed while a procedure is taking place. You need to ask the mandatory question: Can that step be safely eliminated? If not, can its duration be reduced?

As an example, let's assume that you look at the current state in your department and you see that a staff member goes on the hunt for positioning devices during the room cleanup. When she gets to the location where the positioning devices are she finds a jumbled mess that makes the hunt a lot less pleasant and makes it take longer. After the right positioning devices are found, the staff member has to find a cart to transport them, loads the devices, and takes them to the room to start wiping them for the procedure. Can you think of a few alternative ways of dealing with this situation? Could you organize a 7S project on the Positioning Devices Cabinet, so they are all easy to find? How about a dedicated cart for positioning devices parked in a pre-determined location? Could these devices be pre-staged while the prior procedure is taking place? Would it make sense to identify the most common positioning devices and have a cabinet in each OR Suite? The answers you come up with will be a reflection of your department's resources, resourcefulness, team spirit, and desire to improve.

Making Internal steps less taxing

Has it ever happened to you that when you think you are ready to get going with the procedure and are about to take the stroll to pre-surg to get your patient, the Instrument Tech screams "The set is missing a Mayo Clamp" or some other preparatory step that should have taken place before did not happen. Those blood pressure-raising events happen for a variety of reasons, but we tend to immediately look for who to blame, normally under the banner of "accountability". It may very well be that some of your co-workers are slackers, but probably not everybody. Remember that the problem is normally the process, not the people.

Some of these issues will be solved by the use of Changeover Checklists. A Changeover Checklist lists all of the items, staff, and information you need and that must be completed prior to the start of the Internal Changeover steps so as to minimize the time the OR Suite is encumbered in this way. No two changeover checklists are going to be the same, as they are dependent on the department's resources, layout, inventory management techniques, and a host of other issues. A sample checklist could look like the one below.

Ensure that all equipment to be used in the procedure is in proper working order. It would be a tremendous waste of time and a risk to have a piece of equipment not perform according to specs during the procedure. If that could have been prevented with a function check, it makes it all the more critical. So, if you could you develop a function check procedure for all equipment to be staged for the next procedure it will

Changeover Checklist			
Room		8 - Ortho 1	
Procedure		Total Joint	
Physician		Matias Indart	
Date			
Epic Visit Number		323587	
Patient's Last Name		Sidney Crosby	
Check	Changeover Staff - Min of 2 Other staff Member can Flex to assist		
	Robin G	███████	Lynn M
	Nancy R	███████	Joe A
	Case Cart		
	All Hospital's Instrument Trays		
	All Supplier's Instruments Trays		
	Zimmer		
	Striker		
	Other:		
	All Preference peel-packed instruments from Sterile Core		
	Supplies		
	All Supplies in case cart		
	All preference supplies from Sterile Core		
	Sutures		
	Drill bits		
	Extra towels		
	Other:		
	Standard Operating Procedures		
	SOP101 General OR Setup		
	SOP323 Total Joint		

cut down on changeover time while making the unavoidable internal steps a bit less taxing.

One last general consideration is that of transport. In the example above of the staff members obtaining positioning devices, we mentioned having to look for a cart to transport them. As trivial as this may sound, there is a substantial amount of time spent every day looking for transport devices. If you can find a way to have those devices in place at predictable locations, you will make the unavoidable internal steps a bit more efficient.

In conclusion, by separating internal from external steps, the improvements will come from doing as much preparation ahead of time as possible, and not by changing the changeover process itself.

Chapter 4: Knowledge Check

Define Internal Changeover Step

_____

_____

_____

_____

Define External Changeover Step

_____

_____

_____

_____

Separating Internal from External means to shorten the duration of all steps.

☐ True
☐ False

Which of the following tools facilitate the Separating phase:

☐ Changeover Preparedness Checklist
☐ Equipment Functional Checks
☐ Complete Case Carts
☐ A Suture Consignment Program
☐ Optimization of Transportation steps

Chapter 5: Converting Internal Steps to External Steps

Armed with the knowledge of the difference between Internal and External Changeover steps, you went to the OR Suite and started observing. Once you see what is what, you start documenting using the Standard Work Definition, a video camera, or both. Whatever you choose to document the steps of work, make it a standard tool, a blank pad of paper will not do. Then you sit down to review and match your findings on paper versus the video. There is a good chance you will have to go back to the staff members you observed to ask them about some details you may have missed. Once you feel comfortable that you have an accurate reflection of the changeover process on paper you start separating Internal from External steps. Along the way, you see that some steps, if performed in a different sequence, they could save time.

- Staff members may be struggling to transport supplies because you don't have a cart or the cart is nowhere to be found.

- Some steps might simply be eliminated.

- Environmental Services carts may arrive without all the materials needed to perform the cleaning.

- Cleaning procedures may vary greatly from person to person and crew to crew.

- Equipment may not be in proper working condition.

- Incomplete case carts coming into the OR Suite will delay the changeover.

For these initial findings you will have to look at using checklists, checklists of operating conditions, and transport improvements.

There is a very good chance that some of the improvement opportunities you identify during this initial review are outside of your control. Some of these issues may be directly related to the operating procedures in other departments. You may have measured, for example, that in 72% of all changeovers, there is a shortage of supplies. This may be due to the fact that the Materials Management department is still using the obsolete PAR level system. Develop a list of these improvement opportunities and go through the appropriate channels to get them addressed.

Once you worked on the improvement opportunities within your control, you are ready to move to Phase II, converting Internal Changeover steps to External steps. The idea is to choose the lesser of two evils. All changeover is waste. Internal steps are a worse kind of waste because they prevent the OR Suite from being used for procedures. This whole phase is based on your asking the following question:

*How can I convert this Internal step into an
External one?*

External steps are primarily preparatory in nature. So, another way of looking at this is doing more preparation reduces the amount of time the OR Suite is encumbered during the changeover.

Conversion of Internal Steps

In the previous phase you made sure that any step that could be done ahead of time was done. In this phase of the Quick Changeover process you look at the remaining internal steps, and attempt to redesign the process in order to be able to do those steps externally. This will typically require some effect and creativity. Following are some examples of how this might work.

One of the time-consuming internal steps is the setting up of the back table, with all of the instruments and supplies to be used during the surgery. Depending on the complexity of the surgery, this may only take a few minutes or many minutes. If the back table for the next surgery was assembled in a sterile environment ahead of time, this would convert an important internal step into an external one, and reduce the downtime for the OR suite. We recognize that would require a major change in current practice, but this should not discourage your from exploring these more aggressive options.

Another example of converting internal to external steps would be to have the DVT pumps replaced from procedure to procedure, instead of being cleaned inside the room. The replacement pump could be cleaned outside of the OR suite ahead of time.

Be aggressive and question everything. In many cases your ideas may run afoul of current practices and you may have to compromise. Go ahead and compromise, but save the idea in the Continuous Process Improvement database for later review. Some great ideas may not be possible today, but they may be possible in the future.

Standardization

There may be some steps or groupings of steps that are performed differently depending on the person doing the work. Look for ways to keep repeatable features constant from procedure to procedure to eliminate the internal steps. As an example, the location of every piece of equipment, kick bucket, recycling bin, stool, etc should be standard and obsessively maintained to ensure repeatability. If there is something that needs replacing from procedure to procedure ask yourself, "Is there a way to not replace it or to make the replacement time as short as possible?"

Standard Operating Procedures

One of the nemeses of Quick Changeover is the lack of standard procedures for the whole changeover process. The steps from the end of a procedure to the start of the next one must be highly orchestrated. This does not mean they have to be rigid. We all know how many surprises you deal with in the OR on a daily basis. Let's save your energies for those unavoidable surprises, not for the predictable elements. To have a repeatable procedure, document every global step in detail, develop a chart, and train all the staff members involved. Let's take a look at this example:

1. Case Cart is staged with Instruments,

2. Pick disposables to Preference card,

3. Stage Case Cart in OR Suite parking spot (1-16),

4. OR tech moves Case cart to OR Suite,

5. Set up back table,

6. Place all "Hold" items in "Hold/Return Rack" on Sterile Core,

7. Place Case cart outside the OR Suite on Outer Core parking area,

8. OR Nurse picks preference items,

9. Case starts,

10. Case ends,

11. OR Tech brings Case cart back in the OR Suite and loads,

12. OR Tech delivers cart to return area, foams trays, and washes hands,

13. OR Tech starts over from step 4.

This type of written standard procedure will let everyone know what to expect when a case is over, and what are the steps to take when called to action.

It may not always be possible or easy to redesign changeover processes to convert internal steps to external steps, due to a variety of constraints. However this should not discourage you from making an aggressive attempt, for this will result in substantial time saving.

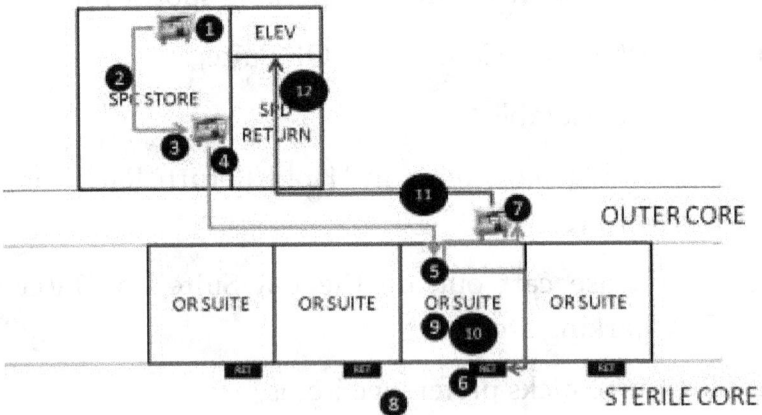

Chapter 5: Knowledge Check

The need to improve OR Suite Changeover can be identified using the following assessment tools:

☐ Value Stream Mapping
☐ Cause and Effect Analysis (Fishbone Diagram)
☐ Direct observation
☐ Staff feedback
☐ All of the above

While the Separating Phase requires changes to the process, the Converting Phase focuses on early preparation.

☐ True
☐ False

Standard Operating Procedures facilitate the Conversion phase:

☐ True
☐ False

Chapter 6: Streamlining Changeover Work Flow

Changeovers are a fact of life. They are waste, but they are also unavoidable. There will be many remaining Internal and External Changeover steps, but hopefully fewer than when you started and much more predictable and standardized. By now, you have improved the OR Suite changeover substantially by separating Internal from External changeover steps;. You then reviewed the internal steps one more time to see which ones can be converted into external steps. You now need to go back over the remaining Internal and External Changeover steps and look for ways to reduce their duration. This last phase, that of reducing the duration of all remaining changeover steps, we call Streamlining all aspects of the Changeover Workflow.

Applying 7S – 5S plus Safety and Security

Knowing where all equipment and supplies should be is specially helpful with External steps, as it eliminates or minimizes any search time that may currently be involved. This is not just "good housekeeping" for it requires a commitment to setting up the area, and also to maintaining all the equipment and supplies locations in a standard manner as identified by the 7S team.

We recommend that the Quick Changeover Team Leader and his/her team identify all the equipment and supplies locations that directly impact changeover and bring in a 7S team to work on those areas one at a time. You may have an equipment room that is messy, unorganized, and unsafe. The same might be true for the Anesthesia room. The supplies you keep in the Sterile core might be difficult to find or require some "hunting" or scavenging the bottom of the drawers.

Before you start a 7S project associated with medical supplies or equipment, you and the department leadership need to get together with staff and let them know this project is about to take place. There are several reasons to be extra cautious in this case. First, messy as it may be, staff is used to it and they may have developed a whole host of work-arounds which you will take away from them. Second, you must put the "hoarders" on notice that you are starting on a path to make supplies problems more evident, so they can be fixed. If they keep their private stashes, some problems go unnoticed and unsolved.

If you think that this 7S stuff is difficult, think about cleaning a messy garage and the steps you would need to go through. You will be very close to the 7S process. Let's give it a try:

You start by staring at the messy garage and, after you go back in the kitchen for another cup of coffee, you take the following steps – notice the "S":

Sort-Take the stuff out to the driveway and make piles

The sorting and the "piles" are the same for the garage as they are for the equipment room. There are some items that you will throw away, some you will keep, some you will donate, and some that are you are not sure. Tag the items you are not sure and disposition within 30 days.

Shine-Clean up the garage while making the piles

Hopefully, you are not doing this alone and someone can fire up the power washer while you are in the driveway sorting items. This process applies also to the anesthesia room. Once it is empty clean it thoroughly and while cleaning all items, inspect them for damage.

Set In Order-Bring the items back in the garage

You are now ready to bring back into the garage all the items you plan to keep, and also a "maybe" pile. The rest will be loaded into the minivan to take to Savers or Goodwill and the rest to the local recycling facility. The same goes for the implants room. You will locate all the items according to frequency of use, weight, size, etc. Educate yourself on some basic ergonomic rules.

Safety and Security Audits

This is a stop along the way, when you bring your Safety and Security teams for a quick audit to make sure that the new arrangements do not impact Safety or Security rules.

Standardize-Making sure it stays that way

How do you make sure that when the kids come back from baseball practice they place their equipment always in the same place? How about preventing the lawnmower from wandering all over the garage? The same goes for the equipment nook in pre-surg. Marking, labeling, and making all the locations clear and unequivocal will facilitate the discipline of putting things back where they belong and can be easily found. But, as you know, if it were only that easy.

Sustain-The commitment to a clean garage

If Dad is the first one to throw the golf bag in a corner, where the dog food goes, because he is in a rush (to watch American Gladiators?) what do you expect from the kids? If Mom walks past the sports equipment rack to see the rack empty and the equipment on the floor and she says nothing, she just condoned this bad behavior. The same goes for the Perioperative Services department as a whole. It is primarily up to the leadership team to ensure that any improvement made under the Lean banner is sustained. Commitment from the leadership team is more than 50% of the battle. The other less-than-50% are the sustainability tools you will find in *7S in the OR* book of this series.

Work in Parallel

Some months ago, one of our associates lead a Changeover project for patient rooms in a Med/Surg unit. Among the many tools used to gather data, they used a "Spaghetti diagram" like the one below which comes from an OR project. This tool shows all the

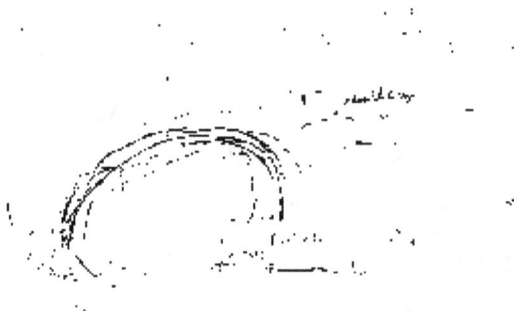

paths a person follows when doing work. They noticed that the person walked around the bed many, many times to make it. One of the ideas the team pondered was "what if we try to do the room changeover with two staff instead of one?" The result was a more-than-proportional reduction in time. The main reason was that a two-person team was able to reduce the walking, as compared to the amount of walking that a single individual is forced to do when working alone. Can the cleaning time be reduced if done as a team in the OR suite? How numerous a team? Beware of the principle of Diminishing Marginal Returns (after a certain point, the more resources you add, the less output you get). Is it worth setting the back table as a team? We cannot give you the answers to these questions because they vary greatly from hospital to hospital and even from OR Suite to OR Suite. Size, layout, location of supplies, and a host of other local issues influence the answers. Start with the questions and do not accept a simple *no* for an answer. Also remember that today's *no* is not a forever *no*.

Automation

Just a few words on this issue, as it is such a tempting way to spend the hospital's money. Remember the case a few lines above about the Patient room changeover project? At another hospital when the Assessment Team made the recommendation to improve patient room changeover, the EVS Director replied dismissively: "All we need is a bed Management System", In other words, automation was *the* solution in the Director's mind.

In our experience with hospitals we have noticed a substantial proclivity to spend heavily on hi-tech items. We are not at all suggesting that any form of automation is bad, but if you do not start with an efficient process, you may be enshrining inefficiencies into a piece of software or an automated piece of equipment which will make it much harder to change. Do not shun automation, just take a very hard look at the process and see what you can get with as little expense as possible.

The main objective of this last Phase in the Quick Changeover process is to optimize each individual changeover step, whether internal or external. To improve your patient throughput and OR suite utilization at this stage, you need to focus on reducing *internal* changeover steps. As you work on streamlining the remaining work steps, you may find additional opportunities to convert internal to external steps, and of course you will want to take advantage of those. In the coming chapters we will be discussing in more detail how materials and standardization effect changeovers.

Chapter 6: Knowledge Check

Streamlining refers to reducing the duration of all the remaining Changeover steps, whether Internal or External.

☐ True
☐ False

7S is a Workplace Organization methodology that supports Quick Changeovers. Place the "S" in the right order:

☐ Set in Order
☐ Security
☐ Standardize
☐ Sort
☐ Shine
☐ Sustain
☐ Safety

By working in parallel, two people can never achieve a more-than-proportional reduction in process time.

☐ True
☐ False

Chapter 7: Quick Changeover and Supplies Management

There is no doubt that supplies are needed and used as a part of the changeover process, and that their proper management can have a positive effect on our changeover time. So first, let's define our terms when we discuss the impact of supplies on Quick Changeover, and make sure you understand the scope of the discussion. You can then move to some suggestions on how to improve this process.

The first category of supplies is the cleaning supplies and chemicals used during the actual OR suite cleanup. Searching or running out of these items will impact our ability to complete our changeover work. The second category is the supplies stored inside the OR suite. Typically you will stock a number of items within the OR suite, not for regular use but for convenience or backup, to be used as needed without having to exit the room during a procedure. Finally, you have a large amount of medical supplies stored within the sterile core, sometimes amounting to several million dollars worth. Our goal for these items, as well as for supplies management in general, is to never have too much or too little, to be able to find what you are looking for easily, and to replenish these supplies efficiently.

The method most commonly used in hospitals to manage supplies is called the "Par Level" method. A quantity of a given item is set, with a target of a certain number of days of supply, based on usage, cost, size and weight, and shelf life. Frequently, often daily, a supplies handler will check on the inventory levels of these items, and refill as needed with the quantity missing, in order to bring the quantity back "up to par".

No world-class organization, outside of hospitals, uses the Par Level method for material management, and for good reason. The method of choice is called Kanban, a Japanese word meaning *signal*. While the Kanban method is similar to the Par method in that you set a target inventory level, it is very different when it comes to the replenishment methodology. In the simplest Kanban method, and there are several, you will divide the total amount into two quantities. You consume one quantity at a time, and only replenish when it has been used. The second quantity is sufficient for our needs while the first one is being refilled.

This way of working has seven main advantages over a Par Level system:

1. No daily counting is needed. You wait for a quantity to be consumed and always replenish the same amount. Not having to count can save hundreds or thousands of hours per year in most hospitals.

2. It reduces the number of resupply trips. Since you wait for a Kanban container to be empty, the number of replenishment trips can be reduced significantly. The number of replenishment cycles can be cut by 50% or more, which can be confirmed with a simulation like the Par Versus Kanban Simulation Toolkit from Flow Publishing.

3. Replenishment quantities are fixed. The refilling process is greatly simplified by eliminating the need for counting required by the Par Level system. If you know ahead of time what the refill quantity will be, the item can be stocked in that quantity.

4. It is easier to manage and improve. By tracking the time between replenishment, the stocking quantities can more easily be refined and adjusted over time. This continuous improvement is more difficult to accomplish if all quantities are refilled daily, in varying quantities.

5. Kanban reduces inventory. Experience proves that, with the same target coverage of supplies, a Kanban system will run with up to 50% less inventory than a Par Level system.

6. It is easier to maintain replenishment discipline. Since they do not have to count all inventory locations, or eye-ball the empty bins, supplies handlers find it easier to identify and refill the

empty bins, thereby substantially reducing the opportunities for shortages.

7. Kanban promotes good inventory management practices, while the Par Level method does not. In fact, counting everything is essentially impossible and very labor intensive, and most par-level users simply "eye-ball" the shelves without counting. Organization and housekeeping, "7S" in Lean Hospital terms, is much easier to maintain.

Unfortunately, in a recent poll done by the Lean Hospital Group, 75% of all hospitals polled were still using the Par Level method exclusively. For all of these reasons previous discussed, however, Kanban should be the method of choice for hospital material management, for much of the material that is procured and managed. The gains in productivity, reduced shortages and reduced inventory represent a multi-billion dollar opportunity for the industry.

Changeover Supplies

Our goal for the management of these supplies is simple: never run out and never have to waste time looking for them. Supplies used directly for a changeover will typically be stocked on a changeover cart, and restocked using a simple Kanban system.

Since two physical containers (to divide the two Kanban quantities) will be unlikely because of space constraints, an alternate visual signal will need to be developed. For example, a spray bottle may have a mark halfway down, and when the fluid goes below the line it is time to refill. Each item to be stocked on the cart will need to be analyzed, and a clear replenishment signal defined.

A secondary supply of these items will need to be stored near the OR suite, but probably outside of the sterile core. In Lean terms we call this the "supermarket", which should be managed with the Kanban method described above. The cart will be restocked from the supermarket, and parking lanes for unused carts will also need to be created. Remember that the replenishment of the carts will take place as an "external" step, as you learned in Chapter 4. Once the changeover starts, the cart should be ready to go with no delay.

OR Suite Supplies and OR Sterile Core Supplies

Our goal for these items is also very simple: the changeover team should never need to deal with these items at all. These supplies should be under Kanban control, and the replenishment signals should be responded to and refilled by the Supplies Management staff. The same Kanban methodology should be used in both areas. A detailed discussion of how to set up a Kanban system is available in our book *Supplies Management in the OR*.

You should not underestimate the impact that supplies management can have on the Quick Changeover process. One of our clients was averaging 20 minutes per changeover in gathering together needed equipment and supplies. You don't need to reinvent the wheel, and supplies management in hospitals is really no different (easier, actually) than other industries. Our mission should be to eliminate the Par Level method altogether, and introduce into the OR the same proven material management methods that are being used around the world with great success.

Chapter 7: Knowledge Check

How is the Par Level method similar to the Kanban method?

- ☐ Both Par and Kanban require counting.
- ☐ Both Par and Kanban set a target quantity to stock for a given item.
- ☐ Both Par and Kanban use visual signals to know when to reorder.
- ☐ Both Par and Kanban require approximately the same effort from supplies handlers.

What should be the role of the Quick Changeover team, when it comes to medical supplies that are stocked in the OR Suite or in the sterile core?

- ☐ The Quick Changeover team should also be responsible for all material restocking within the OR department.
- ☐ The Quick Changeover team should do an audit of supplies during the changeover process, and replenish any items that look low.
- ☐ The Quick Changeover team should not have to do anything at all.
- ☐ The Quick Changeover team should respond to "Kanban" signals and only restock items that have a Kanban card.

Kanban is the method of choice for OR supplies management. What does the Japanese word actually mean?

☐ Continuous Improvement
☐ *Supplies Management* in Japanese
☐ Signal or Sign
☐ Quick Changeover

Chapter 8 Standard Work and Quick Changeover

Frequent travelers gravitate to hotel chains like Marriott and Hilton for a number of reasons. Frequent traveler points are of interest to many. Geographic availability is also a plus. But one of the key reasons for customer loyalty for these chains is consistency of service. When you book a room at a Marriott, you pretty much know what you'll be getting, which is usually pretty good, and it will be consistent from hotel to hotel.

We don't know this for certain, but we would be willing to bet that when a room is cleaned at one of these hotels, it is done the same way every time, and that they have invested considerable effort studying the *one best way* to complete that task. The soap and shampoo is always in the same place, we know where to find the remote control, and the iron and ironing board are close at hand. The result of this type of standardization, therefore, is a more efficient process and happier customers. This is what you need for your OR Suite changeovers as well.

We already discussed in Chapter 3 the need to document the *Current State*, that way that changeovers are done today with warts and all. In that chapter you also saw the standard form that is used to document the work steps, the work times, and the quality considerations related to the work. In this chapter we'll drill deeper, and explain how to document a changeover process in detail.

The method for documenting standard work in the OR is fundamentally simple: go to an OR that is in the process of being changed over, observe the work being done by each person, and document it as a series of sequential tasks or work steps. Then, identify the supplies consumed, and assign them to the task where they are used. Repeat this process for any tools and equipment required for each work element. To document the changeover time, take a sampling of work and time by observing a number of different staff members doing the same tasks. Finally, interview an experienced changeover staff member to identify the accuracy of your documentation, and the quality criteria for each work step.

The Standard Work Definition form will be tailored to the needs of different types of procedures. The columns that are needed on the Standard Work Definition form can vary, and not all of them will be always used. In all cases, however, it is important to document the detailed work steps, the work times, the order of changeover steps and the quality aspects of the work.

Some care needs to be taken when observing and documenting work steps and times. Staff members need to know what is taking place, and the reason for capturing this information. They should help in

STANDARD WORK DEFINITION

Value Stream _____
Process _____
SWD Name _____
Date Created _____
Revision _____

Order	Description of Work Performed	Supplies	N/A Y/N	Divisible Y/N	Int / Ext	Equip. Time	Staff Time	Transp Time	TGM Check	Self-check Description

documenting their own work if possible, which will help reduce their concern that the work steps will not be documented correctly. Depending on the hospital environment and culture, staff members being timed may tend to either slow down (thinking that you're out to reduce their standard time) or speed up (thinking that you are measuring their individual performance). Individuals naturally work at different speeds, so gathering a sample of work times is highly advised.

An important rationale for creating a standard work definition has to do with an evaluation of quality, with an eye to error-proofing the changeover steps. In a perfect world a work step can be performed only one way, the right way, with no possibility for error. If this is not the case and a mistake can be made, Murphy's Law will rule and ways *must* be found to eliminate the possibility of defects, or at least catch the mistake immediately. Mistake-proofing the process, called *Poka Yoke* in Japanese, is always the best choice, and often simple tools or fixtures can go a long way to prevent errors during a changeover. Staff inspection is a requirement in cases where a possibility of error remains. This technique is called a Self-Check. If necessary, this self-inspection step can be supplemented by having another co-worker check the same work step; this is called a TQM Check. By applying both a Self-Check and a TQM Check, each work step subject to variability will have been looked at by two sets of eyes. This technique is called *Check-Do-Check*. Applying these simple and usually inexpensive remedies often has an immediate and powerful beneficial effect on quality.

The next section of the chapter is dedicated to the description of the various data elements needed to complete a changeover Standard Work Definition form. It is important to understand the right level at which to document a changeover, and the right amount of detail to include in this form. Too much detail can be as bad as too little. The Standard Work Definition should be a practical document, and provide information that can actually be used.

Header Information

The first data required ties the SWD to a specific type of changeover. You are also documenting the work for a specific type of job category (nurse, tech, etc.), so both of these data elements must be included at the top of the form. The date that the SWD was created is important, as well as the documenter's name.

Work Elements and Task Descriptions

The most basic element of the Standard Work Definition is the description of the work step itself. The task description should be sufficiently detailed to clearly describe the work step, while at the same time keeping the wording concise. Write these tasks in a way that can be understood by most people. Put yourself in the shoes of a new staff member and ask "Is this understandable?" Keep work elements as short as possible without documenting individual motions.

Order

The order is the sequence in which the tasks should be done. This column defines the sequential nature of work in a process. The work steps within a process are normally performed one after the other, but there may be exceptions, especially when documenting a process with more than one labor resource working at the same time and location.

Supplies

It is important to capture this detailed supplies-related information at the same time that the standard work elements are being documented. Otherwise you will need to do it later, and you may miss items. Include here the item number (used by hospital supply personnel), the quantity, and also the item description (used by nurses and staff).

NVA (Y/N)

This column on the form is a Yes/No classification of the work step, as either adding value or not adding value. In a real sense *all* changeover is non-value-adding work, since you are not actually providing medical services while you are preparing a room. That point aside, however, there are work steps that clearly contribute to the completion of the changeover, and steps that do not. Looking for equipment, for example, may be a step that is needed in the Current State, but which can be targeted for elimination in the future.

Divisible

This is another Yes/No data element that asks the question, "Can the work step be performed by more than one person, i.e. shared or broken up?" This knowledge can be helpful in smoothing out the work flow, and assigning the proper number of tasks to each changeover team member.

Internal and External (I/E)

We discussed in a previous chapter the different between an external step and an internal one. Use this column to classify each step accordingly. The Standard Work Definition therefore becomes an important input to the Phase I Separating Internal and External steps.

Work Content Time

Time estimates will need to be measured and documented for each task. This is accomplished by observing the work being performed, and timing the work with different staff members, and gather fresh information through direct observation.

Note that you are separating machine and labor time. Our expectation is that most of the time will be labor-based, but if equipment is used as a part of the changeover, those times will be documented in a separate column, since they can be different from the labor times.

Transport

Document in this column the distance traveled, when transportation is required. Use a consistent Unit of Measure, like feet, yards or meters. Transportation is a non-value-adding activity, so this information will also be useful in improving the changeover process.

Self-Check Description

A Self-Check is an inspection step that is documented on the Standard Work Definition when an element of work contains process variability, i.e. it is possible for the work to be performed incorrectly. The Self-Check is the responsibility of the staff member who has actually done the work. Part of the changeover training process is to ensure that any required quality checks are clearly understood and are able to be performed correctly.

As you complete a SWD you will ask yourself many times: do I need to document quality criteria for this task? The first objective is to eliminate changeover process variability. Process variability usually means having many different ways to do the work, while only one is the correct or best one. Follow this rule: you must document quality criteria against a task *every time there is more than one way possible to do the task, but only one is correct.* The consistent use of this data within the context of the Check-Do-Check technique can yield great results in workmanship quality levels.

TQM Check

This is a second inspection that is performed to validate that an element of work has been completed correctly. The TQM Check is the responsibility of another person on the changeover team. If errors are found in the work step (by the second person), the person that originally did the work must remedy the problem. Note that the person who originally performed the work should have done a Self-Check as well, but often the person doing the work will overlook a mistake that a fresh set of eyes can see. This is the reason why you need a second person to perform a quality check, and cannot rely on just one set of eyes.

Requiring two checks indicates that this work step is critical enough to require an inspection by a second person, and that an error on this step is never acceptable. This check would, of course, be completed before performing any other work steps in the changeover process.

The Check-Do-Check technique builds on the common knowledge that two sets of eyes checking same task are more likely to catch mistakes than just one. An illustration of this is the practice of proof-reading written material. It is always much more likely that somebody other than the author will catch typos and mistakes.

It is a known fact that even a person *trying* to do a good job will make mistakes. As Deming instructed in Point 10, slogans like "Do it right the first time" are useless. A person *trying* to do a good job will still make mistakes at a certain rate, depending on the difficulty of the work and the number of repetitions.

These simple quality tools are a powerful way to mistake-proof a changeover process. The predictable and consistent application of the Check-Do-Check technique puts the staff members on alert to pay attention to and identify opportunities for improvement in the way the work is conducted.

Writing Standard Work Definition

When documenting Standard Work for your OR Suite Changeover, let your common sense guide you. Be realistic with the task times. Lean is not intended to be a labor reduction or labor efficiency program per se. Productivity gains and shorter changeover times will come as a result of a focus on the elimination of non-value-adding steps, and not by rushing.

What level of detail is appropriate for the work steps on the Standard Work Definition form for OR Suite Changeover? If you get too detailed, with only seconds per task, you will end up with too many work steps and a daunting documentation job. A 45 minute changeover documented in 10 second increments will result in 270 discrete work steps and a book the size of *Gray's Anatomy*. Lack of detail, on the other hand, will not give you sufficient visibility of improvement opportunities, and the quality aspects of the work. For our OR changeover, measuring work tasks in minutes is sufficient and the right level of detail. Applying common sense to the level of process documentation detail needed can be an important success factor in being able to improve the process, and in being able to complete our analysis of the Current State in a timely fashion.

A very useful tool to consider is the video camera, as mentioned in Chapter 3. Video recording a staff member during a changeover for the purpose of documenting Standard Work Definitions can be very powerful. The video gives you the ability to review as many times as you need to get the best possible description of the work, look at the work element's nuances, and the times are recorded for you, with no need for a stop watch! Furthermore, when video is used in a controlled environment, you can have an experienced staff member explain what she/he is doing as the work is being performed. This can also be a powerful training tool. On the downside, though, if you think that having a stopwatch-bearing industrial engineer looking over your shoulder is distracting, think about the impact a video camera can have! This is not an insurmountable hurdle. It will just test how well you communicated with the OR staff about the goals of a Lean project.

There is no doubt that documenting the OR changeover Current State can take a substantial amount of time. What happens to the idea of "Rapid Improvement" if you're spending all your time documenting Standard Work? There really isn't a good shortcut for understanding the processes in detail, so be prepared to bite the bullet and get this step completed, well in advance of an actual Kaizen event.

Consider how to communicate the Standard Work to the staff members that will actually be doing the work. This chapter has presented a document, the SWD, describing every step of work, its sequence, the supplies and equipment required, the time it takes to perform the work, and instructions on how to perform the work correctly. Every person must follow the SWD when performing an OR suite changeover. Will you require staff members to read the SWD every time they do a changeover? Certainly not. The Standard Work Definition will become the main training document and be instituted as the policy/procedure for OR suite changeovers. For daily use you should provide some graphical means to quickly glance at the work steps and quality steps, as a checklist, or will just a reminder of the quality steps be enough?

Doing a thorough job of documenting the current state, for each type of labor resource and for each type of changeover (there will be several) provides a strong foundation for the process improvement work that will follow. In the closing chapters we will discuss how to track the performance of the changeover improvements, some examples and the applications of the Kaizen method as the main continuous improvement tool.

Chapter 8: Knowledge Check

Poka Yoke is a Lean Japanese term that means:

- ☐ "Slow Learner" or "Cement Head". Poka = slow and Yoke = rustic person.
- ☐ "Reminder", especially of quality-related issues.
- ☐ Error-Proofing, the elimination of errors.
- ☐ Continuous Improvement

Aviation has an excellent track record of safety, and there were no commercial aviation fatalities in 2010. What is one of the important ways they have achieved this?

- ☐ By weeding out the "bad apples" in the barrel, and firing all low-performers.
- ☐ Through the skillful use of quality slogans and banners in all work areas and in the cockpit.
- ☐ Through the use of checklists for all critical procedures.
- ☐ Through holding people strictly accountable for quality, and following up with rewards and punishments.

What is the title of the form that we use to document Standard Work?

☐ The Standardization Form

☐ The Standard Work Definition Form

☐ The Work Steps Analysis Form

☐ The Analysis of Work, Times and Quality by Process Form

Chapter 9: Measuring Performance and Visual Controls

Back in the early days of aviation, pilots would look over the side of the plane to figure out where they were. Barnstormers would literally fly along the major highways, and follow roadmaps to avoid getting lost. Imagine then, with today's sophisticated aviation technology, asking the pilot "Where are we?" or "How fast are we flying?" and getting the answer "I'm not sure." You'd be looking for your parachute.

The same logic applies to our OR Changeover initiative. You need to be using a dashboard that tells you how fast you are going, how much fuel you are using, and when you can expect to arrive at your destination. Without the appropriate controls you are flying blind. This chapter takes a look at some of the visual controls that can help you in sustaining high OR changeover performance, and discusses some of the basic measurements you will want to have.

One word of caution: you don't want to add a large number of measurements and tools that you don't actually use or need. Every measurement requires data collection, input, analysis and action, and if you have too many you will simply get tired after awhile and stop measuring. It's more important to select a few measures and keep it up, as opposed to being overly ambitious with our measurement goals and having the entire effort collapse.

Measuring Changeover Time

The first and the most important measurement is the actual changeover time. The clock starts ticking when the previous procedure ends and the patient has left the OR suite, and the clock stops when the room is ready for the next procedure. The next procedure may not start immediately, however, but that idle time is not considered a part of the changeover time.

If you are using a computer system to track our performance, you need to make sure that these two times are recorded properly. We have heard of systems that will accurately record the start time for the changeover, but not capture the completion time, instead only recording the start of the next procedure and not when the OR suite was actually ready. The actual changeover time will be inaccurate and inflated in this case.

So what if you don't have a database, or the electronic system is not collecting data the way you would like? Your first recourse should be the Information Services department, to see if there is a way to use the existing computer resources that you're not yet aware of. There may be some lesser-known features or workarounds, or even some minor customization, that can provide you what you need without going outside of the existing data collection system. That failing you may need to create a manual logbook.

Previous generations had to do this to collect data, so you can too if necessary.

What is not acceptable is to not measure changeover time, even when you feel that it has been optimized. It is always possible to backslide, and if you don't measure it, how would you know? The measurement of OR changeover time is not a temporary metric, it's a permanent one.

Not all OR changeovers are the same, so you also need to classify each changeover in accordance with its type. For example, you may have minor changeovers (after a cataract surgery, for example), medium changeovers (after a lap chole, for example) or a major changeover (after orthopedic spinal procedure, for example). You need to classify your changeovers by type, along with recording the actual changeover time. Don't make it too complex; high, medium and low may be sufficient.

Other Measurements

What else might you want to measure, keeping in mind the recommendation to keep it simple? Adding another measurement is not a bad thing if the data is easily available or already being collected. Here are some ideas for other OR Changeover performance measurements:

- Number of Supplies Shortages. Number of times per reporting period that the changeover was delayed due to lack of supplies.

- Equipment Shortages. Number of times per reporting period that needed equipment was not immediately available.

- Number of Case Cart Errors. Number of times that the changeover was delayed due to errors or shortages on the case cart.

- Number of Understaffing Incidents. If you have designed the process for three people, but only have two for a changeover, it will obviously take longer. How many times a week does this happen?

- Restocking of OR Supplies. Supplies kept within the OR should never need to be restocked by the changeover personnel. If this need does arise, keep track of it.

The Poker Chip Data Collection Method

If the data is too hard to collect, people won't do it. Here's a suggestion for a simple way to gather data manually without placing a high burden on the folks doing the work. Provide a small number of different colored poker chips, with each color representing a different type of error. Red, for example, may represent a supplies shortage, while green may be an equipment shortage. If and when these errors occur, simply place a poker chip of the correct color in a collection bowl. Count up the different colors at the end of each week, and enter it into a spreadsheet. Caution: check with Infection Control about the use of this method within the sterile core!

The Status Light

Have you ever walked by an empty OR Suite and wondered what was happening in there? Was it ready for the next procedure? Was it waiting to be set up? A status light can be helpful in signaling the status of the room, with a specific color signaling that the room is being changed over, another color signaling that it is ready for use, and yet another color to signify that it is in use. By the way, the traditional color for changeover in manufacturing, if there is such a tradition, is the color blue.

The Changeover Clock

We emphasized, but let's say it again, that our goal is not to reduce changeover time by rushing (and potentially increasing errors). That said, there is something healthy about being aware of the passage of time while working on a changeover, and what we have done in some cases is install a large digital clock that can count down or up. The clock is in an easily seen place, or maybe even mounted to a changeover cart, and it acts as a reminder that the "clock is ticking". We recommend a clock that is counting up from zero instead of a countdown clock that starts with the "budgeted" amount of time and counts down to zero. Setting a goal will become a self-fulfilling prophesy. For example, you may be able to complete a changeover in 20 minutes with the help of a countdown clock, but chances are you won't get any better.

Sharing Results

Results of actual changeover times, by type, should be graphed and displayed in the OR area, along with other important OR performance data. We're assuming that the raw data is being collected, but there also needs to be an owner of the data who will also have the responsibility for updating the graph and posting the results at least monthly. This is not secret information, and if you are continually improving then the graph can be a way to show off.

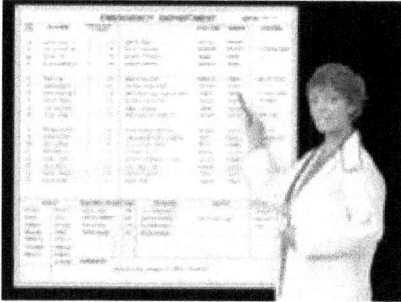

If you are backsliding, i.e. changeover times are increasing, the public graph can help to motivate some additional process improvement.

The bottom line is that you need to put measurements and accountability in place to help you avoid backsliding, i.e. going back to the way it used to be prior to the improvements. Sustaining process improvements requires a concerted effort, and will not happen by itself. Without a Lean Management System, of which measurements are a part, the sustainability rate for process improvements is depressingly low. You don't want that to happen to you.

Chapter 9: Knowledge Check

True or False: In accordance with Lean Thinking, the more measurements of a process, the better.

☐ True
☐ False

One visual tool for capturing data is the use of poker chips to represent different types of problems. What advantages does the poker chip method have?

☐ It is easy to use.
☐ It is visual and color coded.
☐ It is easy to understand.
☐ All of the above.

What is a common slogan related to performance measurement?

☐ What Gets Measured Gets Done
☐ A Stitch In Time Saves Nine
☐ Go To The Gemba
☐ Quality Is Job One
☐ Change We Can Believe In

Chapter 10: Revolution in the OR

We want to give you a taste of the opportunities that await you when you decide to start applying the tools and techniques of Quick Changeover to your OR. These tools are to be applied within the largest context of a Lean initiative across the entire Perioperative Services department. Conventional wisdom, which the authors support, is that these tools and any Lean tools should be applied within the context of a hospital-wide Lean initiative. But the Perioperative Services department is one of two exceptions in a hospital, along with the Emergency Department, that operate with a higher degree of autonomy and can embark on a Lean journey of its own and be more successful than a Nursing Unit would be if it tried to go it alone.

There is a very good chance that the issue of "Slow Changeovers" was identified as an opportunity for improvement during a Value Stream Mapping event for the whole Perioperative Services department, or by surgeons feedback, or by a staff member commenting on his/her experience at St. Elsewhere, or by hospital leadership as the result of benchmarking. Whatever the triggering event, improving the OR Suite changeover process is what you have been tasked to do.

A word on benchmarking before we proceed. The authors are all for benchmarking as one more piece of the puzzle, but not as the only objective for the Changeover Improvement team. If your goal is to be only as good as the next guy, you are not pursuing *perfection*, a symptom that the Lean principles have not yet permeated your hospital or Perioperative Services Department's culture.

Following are a few examples of Kaizen projects aimed at improving OR Suite changeover times.

The Problem: Too Many Case Carts

A common practice among Sterile Processing departments is to pick case carts well ahead of the actual need, normally one day ahead. This is done for a variety of reasons, from staffing patterns to confusing departmental structures.

The issue was identified during a Value Stream Mapping session as:

> *"It takes several minutes to wade through the sea of case carts to get to the one I need. Especially after they have been jumbled by the first cases of the day."*

The solution: Cut the number of case carts staged in half and go from there

Start picking case carts as close as possible to the time of use. This is easier said than done, as the parked case carts provide a sense of security to the OR staff. The solution was applied in steps:

Step 1: Pick one half day of procedures in advance, instead of the whole day.

Step 2: Stage the next case next to the OR Suite with clear signals indicating "Next Case"

Step 3: Monitor compliance and performance by tracking Case Cart shortages per week/month and continue reducing the case cart picking window.

The benefits: Average of 3 to 5 minutes per changeover, of internal time.

The Problem: Supplies Shortages

This is a pervasive problem across many ORs. The ones that do not report supplies problems rotate their inventories at glacial speeds, (which is really slow).

This issue was identified during a preparation meeting with the entire Perioperative Services Department staff:

"We never have the supplies we need"

Chasing and hunting for supplies delays the OR Suite changeover by many minutes. Upon further examination, we realized that this was primarily based on the correct perception that the inventory management methods to supply the department with medical supplies were completely broken. Since there was no data, a short project to track supplies shortages was put in place to ascertain the magnitude of the problem. The staff was right. The average number of shortages per day was 17.

The solution: Implement two-bin Kanban This method is discussed in Chapter 8 and in-depth in *Supplies Management in the OR*. The steps applied in this case:

- Benchmark metrics. Shortages and Inventory turns.

- Create a database of OR supplies.

- Identify usage by supply. This step can be tricky, as many hospitals do not have a perpetual inventory system.

- Perform initial Kanban calculations.

- Round the Kanban calculations to match the most reasonable quantities, like whole package sizes. e.g. full suture boxes.

- Develop a full replenishment profile for every supply in the database or "A Plan for Every Part".

- Acquire shelving units and bins as needed. Try very hard to use what you have.

- Design labels, print labels, fill bins, fill carts/shelves.

- Train staff

- Develop and archive Kanban policy.

A simple example of this method was the "Suture

Wall". For the more popular types of sutures, an inventory of two boxes was established, with one box on top of the other. The rule is "You only consume from the top box" Whenever a staff member takes the last unit from a box, the box is placed on the top shelf. That empty box is the replenishment signal. The Materials Specialist brings a full box on his next "milk run" and places it under the box in use in the right location.

The benefits: a reduction of 10 to 12 minutes of hunting time per changeover, with some internal time and some external time. As a side note, the shortages per day were virtually eliminated and the inventory was reduced by more than $500,000.

The Problem: Internal Cleaning Time

During the observation phase of the internal changeover steps, cleaning was major factor. From the actual cleaning time to the chemical dwell time, all these steps are primarily internal steps and require careful consideration.

The realization that the cleaning procedure could be improved came from the "spaghetti diagrams" created for the cleaning procedure. It revealed that one person had to walk many times in and out of the OR Suite to reach the cleaning cart. The cleaning cart was not organized in the order of use, requiring multiple turns around the cart.

Also, the team tested cleaning the OR Suite with more than one person. With two staff members, the time was cut in more than half. This solution was an onerous one, however, due to staffing constraints. For emergency situations, team cleaning would be used.

The solution: Standardize the cleaning procedure and implement team cleaning for stats

To standardized the cleaning procedure, the team created a detailed Standard Work definition (SWD) of the cleaning steps with sequence, times, and quality checks. This SWD also includes all the materials necessary to do the job.

The benefits: 3 minutes of cleaning time eliminated, all internal steps.

The Problem: The Shift Change Meeting

The shift change meeting is an institution at almost every hospital. During this time the world stops and the patient appears to no longer be a priority. The team noticed that during shift change, there was no Environmental Services staff to be found on the floor as they all have to attend the shift change meeting on the hospital's bottom floor. These meetings were supposed to take 30 minutes, but add walk time back and forth (plus a bit of socializing) and you are out of luck for 45 minutes. Some of us attended a couple of these meetings to verify that no information was exchanged that required physical presence.

The solution: Eliminate Shift Change Meetings

Since eliminating the meeting at once was perceived as too drastic, the Environmental Services team started by reducing the number of meetings held. The meeting was no longer named the "Shift Change" meeting but the "Staff meeting" The frequency was first cut in half and then the duration was gradually reduced. This required the development of a communications strategy by the Environmental Services leadership.

The benefit: 8 EVS staff x 45 min/day x 365 days/year = 2,190 hrs/year (approximately one full FTE worth of work).

These are just a few examples of the possibilities to be uncovered through the application of the Quick Changeover methodology and the Kaizen spirit. When you achieve similar or better results than the ones described in the examples above, feel free to share your results with us, and remember that Continuous Improvement is never ending. In the last chapter we briefly discuss Lean's main tool for continuous improvement, Kaizen.

Chapter 10: Knowledge Check

Supply shortages can only be measured in the OR by implementing dedicated software.

☐ True
☐ False

Solutions from other hospitals can be copied directly, as all ORs are the same.

☐ True
☐ False

All staff is delivering value during the Shift Change Meeting

☐ True
☐ False

Chapter 11: Kaizen in the OR

Here's how a typical improvement project gets managed in many hospitals. A need to improve arises, either as a suggestion or more likely as the result of a fire, like a negative Joint Commission survey finding. A committee is formed, and the group gets together periodically to work on the issue. Months later, little progress has been made, and much of each meeting time is simply getting back up to speed on what was discussed at the previous meeting. Or, if the urgency is high, a "tiger team" is organized to get the problem fixed once and for all. Lacking a clear methodology and training in problem solving, the team struggles as the clock ticks. As you may surmise, we are not big fans of these approaches.

We address in detail the Lean approach to process improvement in our companion book *Kaizen in the OR*. In this short chapter we'll give you an introduction to the recommended way to organize process improvement projects, including a Quick Changeover effort covered in this book. The word Kaizen means "Continuous Improvement" in Japanese, and describes an attitude of striving towards perfection, usually through a series of small but continuous changes in a process. When we are referring to a group effort over a period of time, we use the term *Kaizen Event*, which is a focused activity of between 3 to 5 days, with a small team of people, with the goal of improving a process within that time.

The keys to the success of the Kaizen Event method are *process*, *training* and *focus*. Let's take a look are each of these points one by one.

Process means that you are following a proven series of steps to organize a Kaizen event, to staff it correctly, to manage the 3 to 5 day activity, to document and report on the new process, and to ensure sustainability of the changes. A Kaizen Event follows a daily, and sometimes hourly, schedule and the team understands that there are non-optional goals for the event that must be met. The role of the team leader is to keep the event on track and on schedule. The Kaizen event is focused on doing, not on brainstorming only. If the end of the event arrives and the ideas have not been implemented, this cannot be considered a successful activity.

Training means that you are not only trying to be smart, but you are also applying a set of proven methods and tools to the problem or opportunity, in this case the reduction of changeover times in the OR. A Kaizen event is an active application of the scientific method, whereby you develop a hypothesis, you test the hypothesis in a controlled environment, you evaluate the results and you take the appropriate action. The continuous improvement model is called PDCA (Plan, Do, Check, Act), an acronym that may be familiar to you. While our solutions are not simply copies of techniques that have been done elsewhere,

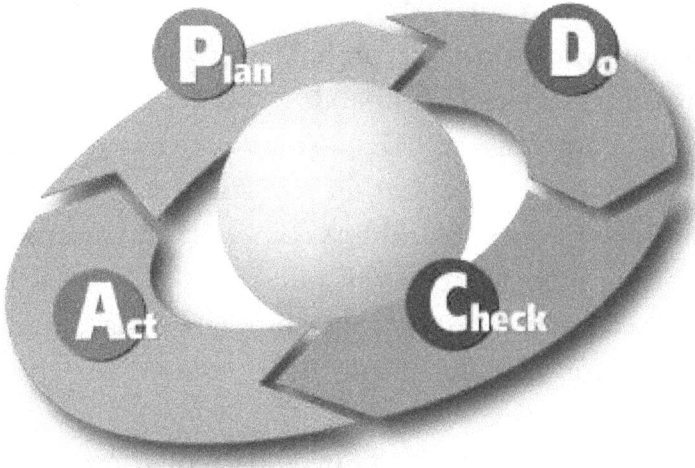

you don't need to reinvent the wheel either, and the Lean toolkit is full of proven methods that may work for you also.

Most of the training in a Lean culture does not take place in the classroom, but rather in the "gemba", the place where the work is actually done. In the case of a Quick Changeover Kaizen event, some formal training will be needed but the bulk of the training will occur in the process of doing: documenting the current state, applying the three stages of Quick Changeover, and implementing and formalizing the new process. A mentor, someone who has been through the process before, is necessary, and for that reason outside Lean consultants are often used to get started. Eventually, of course, the hospital staff will need to take the Lean ball themselves and run with it.

The third key to success is focus, and this may be the most important one. It's probably always been true, but it seems especially true today: we all suffer from a form of organizational ADD. We have so many things clamoring for our attention constantly, from our emails, cell phones, Blackberrys, co-workers, internet, regulatory agencies, and on and on. It's no wonder that it takes forever to actually complete a task. Some organizations actually create "safe rooms" for their employees, places where they can work uninterrupted, for at least for a part of the day, in order to actually get something done. A Kaizen event takes this approach. Everyone on the team understands that while they are on the team, their regular jobs are on hold, or are being back-filled by a co-worker. They have the "luxury" but also the obligation to focus 100% on the Kaizen goal. With that approach, it is amazing what can be accomplished. Problems that have lingered for months or even years can be resolved in a few days.

Your *Quick Changeover in the OR* project should use this method. There is a significant amount of preparation work that needs to be done, especially with the documentation of the Current State. Once this preparation has been completed, however, design the new changeover process in a few days, probably with a 5 day Kaizen event, and begin to enjoy the benefits of Quick Changeover immediately.

One last comment before we send you on your way. Shigeo Shingo recommended doing a Quick Changeover Kaizen in the same area more than once, and reported a continual reduction in the changeover time after every event. So don't think that after one event you are done. Kaizen means continual improvement, and there is no end to the opportunities for improvement.

Chapter 11: Knowledge Check

What is the biggest advantage of the Kaizen approach to process improvement?

- ☐ Changes get done in a short amount of time.
- ☐ Team members are able to focus, and are dedicated to the project.
- ☐ The Kaizen improvement process is formal and well-defined.
- ☐ All of the above.

The Lean approach to training includes the following approach and philosophy:

- ☐ Learn primarily by doing.
- ☐ Learning is hard, so it's necessary to study hard.
- ☐ You have to memorize before you can understand.
- ☐ Rely on the "sensei" (lean mentor) for good ideas for improvement.

Put the following Kaizen event steps in the correct order.

☐ Follow up and Sustain
☐ Create Report
☐ Run Event
☐ Assign Roles
☐ Prepare

Leonardo Group Americas LLC (LGA)

The authors are the Principals with Leonardo Group Americas, LLC.

The mission of *Leonardo Group Americas* is to assist its hospital clients to achieve success with the implementation of advanced Lean methods. This is accomplished through our talented staff and their profound knowledge and experience, a suite of world-class training seminars, state of the art web-based training, certification programs, books and materials, and through the prudent application of Lean software tools.

LGA has been involved with the deployment of Lean in hospitals since 2002, and is a founding member of the Lean Hospital Group. They have conducted Lean improvement projects in virtually every hospital process and Value Stream.

Find out more about Leonardo Group Americas at
www.leonardogroupamericas.com
and
www.leanhospitalgroup.com

or send us an email at
contact@leonardogroupamericas.com.